Rangers

The eyes and ears
of the Peak National Park

Yorkshire Art Circus
1998

Published by **Yorkshire Art Circus**, School Lane, Glasshoughton,
Castleford, West Yorkshire, WF10 4QH Tel: 01977 550401 Fax: 01977 512819
e-mail admin@artcircus.org.uk

Editing team: Geoff Frost, Neville Care, Anna Wharton, Jo Henderson, Ian Daley.

Production: Ian Daley, Lorna Hey, Rosie Nixon and typists.

Photographs: Ray Manley and the Peak National Park Authority.

Cover design: Paul Miller of Ergo Design

Printed by FM Repro, Roberttown, Liversedge.

ISBN:1 898311 36 6

Classification: Social History, Photography.

Our thanks to all the Peak Park Rangers who played a part in creating this book, to Anna
Wharton for overseeing the project and to John Cree who started it all off.

British Library Cataloguing in Publication Data.
A catalogue record for this book is available from the British Library.

Yorkshire Art Circus is a unique book publisher. We work to increase access to writing and
publishing and to develop new models of practice for arts in the community. Please write to us
for details of our full programme of workshops and our current book list.

Yorkshire Art Circus Web Site: www.artcircus.org.uk

Yorkshire Art Circus is supported by

We live on a tiny island that over the last hundred and fifty years has been turned from a green and pleasant land into a largely industrial, urban, smoky, choking, brick, concrete and steel land with bits of green in between.

Almost sixty million people live on this little raft and the green bits are our lungs.

One of them is the Peak Park. It is a place I know full well. My first days camping out were spent at Pots and Pans in the Northern Peak and many of my finest days have been spent in Kinder and Bleaklow. The White Peak with its bone white crags and sweet green grass has called me out into the hills over and again. Without these green spaces, I would be lost and so would many millions more.

Keeping watch over them are a group of men and women who, like Aragorn in *Lord of the Rings*, get on with it quietly, trying to keep it good for the rest of us.

I applaud them. May this book celebrate them.

Mike Harding
Dentdale
1998

Geoff Frost

Eric Wood

Neville Care

Steve Bell

Tony Hood

Ian Taylor

Gordon Miller

Adrian Dobb

Hazel Winder

Andy Pollock

Andy Farmer

Andy Valentine

Richard Gregory

Arthur Smith

Lynn Burrow

Dave Roebuck

Andy McGraw

David Mansfield

Gavin Bell

David Pickering

Harry Ball

Doug Kirwen

Graham Phillips

Dr. L A Pearson

Tom Lewis

Gary Hannan

Peter Slack

Jan Cave

Ray Slack

Jeff Cheetham

Andrew Haddon

Jim Collis

Bill Dorely

Julie Frederick

Neil Hanshaw

Ken Sloan

Sheila McHale

Margaret Bailey

Mo Morton

Margaret Black

Johnie Lees

Marion McEwen

Ian Hall

Mike Perks

Clive Smith

Mrs. M Fiengold

William Gregory

Professor Tarn

Belinda Nield

Raff Tuccillo

Mrs Ewers

Ron McLaughlin

Gary Short

Roy Williamson

Terry Agg

Sean Prendergast

Jack Shaw

Sharon Frost

Don & Jean Snoopy

Sheila & Terry Ashton

George Challenger

James Bradbury

Muriel Smith

Sue Frost

Derek Nobles

Julie Cook

Karen Barlow

Ken Hammond

Margaret Baily

Ann & Ray Bell

Jim Collins

Dave Tier

Anna Wharton

John Pearson

This book started as one thing and grew into something else. It began as a Local Distinctiveness training session at Losehill Training Centre and grew into a three day training course for the Peak National Park Ranger Service. It then thought about being a small book cum booklet - by rangers, for rangers - and then matured into a full scale book - by rangers, for the rest of the world. We realised, once the first batch of writing came in, that these stories were quite exceptional and gave an insider's answer to the question 'what does a ranger do'.

Having decided to produce a proper book, we set up an editing team; Anna Wharton, Geoff Frost and Neville Care from the Ranger Service, Ian Daley and myself from the Art Circus. The training sessions had already produced the first batch of stories. The editing team did some more interviewing, edited the existing stories and wrote some new ones themselves. The National Park Authority Archives provided the photos.

A ranger's job is one of the most coveted in the country, although reading through descriptions of hazardous weather conditions, stroppy visitors, recalcitrant animals and human tragedies, you might wonder why. I hope the following stories will provide the answer. This book will give you an insight into what the job is all about, the people the rangers deal with, things they get up to themselves, the drama, monotony, frustration, delight and above all, the satisfaction that comes from working in one of the most beautiful National Parks in the country.

Jo Henderson
Yorkshire Art Circus

FROM PAST TO PRESENT

It seems somewhat bizarre that in 1954, Britain's first National Park Warden Service was inaugurated outside the Nag's Head pub in Edale. Bizarre because its first full-time warden, Tom Tomlinson was a lifelong teetotaller.

Tom had already been a Youth Hostel warden for ten years when he was appointed as the first Chief Warden (now called 'ranger') of the Peak District National Park. The Park's management board at that time was not quite sure what the job should involve. Certainly patrolling the moors was a high priority. There had been new agreements with landowners to allow public access onto their private land and the board was keen to see that this worked satisfactorily.

Tom was told he would have to walk about twenty miles a day, mainly on the moors above Edale. He was tall, strong and exceptionally fit so this proved no problem to him. However, when the board offered him a motorcycle as a mode of official transport he argued that it would not be suitable as he might have to carry injured walkers. They then offered him a motorcycle with a sidecar, again he thought this would not be a good means of transport and eventually he managed to persuade them that a Land Rover would be a much better choice.

The job was especially difficult in those days. There were no precedents to follow. The local farming community was naturally suspicious of an officer appointed by the new National Park. Tom lived some miles away in Hathersage and it took great skill and diplomacy for the Warden Service to become recognised and trusted amongst the locals. Later this became easier when a second warden, George Garlick, was appointed and went to live in Edale, thus becoming part of that community.

The selection process for becoming a volunteer warden was basic but effective. One particular test involved a hill climb. Gordon Miller (presently an Area Ranger) recalls the trial that took place.

"I had become interested in becoming a warden following a talk given by Tom at my school. At 15 years old, I was too young at the time but they let me join as a cadet. Anyone who wanted to become a volunteer had to go out with Tom and prove they were capable. This was done by following him up a gruelling climb to the edges of Kinder Scout. Tom walked at a deceivingly leisurely gait but with enormous, long strides. You had to be really fit to keep up with him. At the top, if you sat down beside him, despite being breathless, he would accept you as a warden. If you were still struggling up the slope he would ask you to come back and try again when you had become fit."

Those were pioneering days. Most walkers wore heavy boots with clinkers and had clothing that had been purchased from ex-army stores. There were no breathable fabrics and no fancy high-tech equipment. Mountain rescue was not efficiently organised like today and there were few civilian teams. The first major change in the Warden Service came in 1960 when it was decided to employ paid part-time wardens. The wardens at that time were mostly made up from rambling clubs and other allied voluntary bodies. They were very much against giving payment to wardens as they thought it might attract the wrong sort of people.

In the winter of 1967/8, a nation-wide outbreak of Foot & Mouth disease caused havoc throughout the country. During this time, the Warden Service gained much respect and goodwill amongst the local farming community by manning roadside checkpoints and generally assisting in the emergency. In the areas bordering the National Park there were 1,154 outbreaks of the disease, whereas in the Park itself there were only 13.

More appointments were made over the following years. Johnny Lees, an Ex-RAF Mountain Rescue team leader and holder of the George Medal, became a training officer. The full-time wardens were sent on Mountain Leadership courses. Volunteers had to attend comprehensive training courses that included navigation and hillcraft. On the trails in the Southern District however, some of the wardens were also trained in horsemanship in order to continue patrols on Mutley - the Warden Service horse.

In 1974, Colonel Eric Bardell, a one time Chief Instructor at the Royal Military Academy, Sandhurst, was appointed as Chief Ranger. The rather custodial sounding name of 'warden' was changed to 'ranger' and the service expanded to cover the whole of the 555 square miles of the National Park. Up to that time, armbands and a badge had been used as means of a warden's identity. The service began to take on a more professional identity and uniforms of lovat-green and Derbyshire tweed were issued to full-time and seasonal rangers. The idea met with success and some part-time and volunteer rangers began to purchase their own breeches and sweaters.

During the following years there were several outbreaks of large moorland fires. One of the worst times was in 1976, when rangers dealt with eighty-two fires in a period of nine weeks. Fire-fighting training and equipment was increased and improved. An All-Terrain Vehicle was purchased to help ferry equipment across the peat bogs and wilderness areas. The late 1970s witnessed the arrival of hunt saboteurs who came to disrupt the traditional grouse shoots. Rangers found themselves caught in the middle of the conflict between the saboteurs and the shooters. By using tact and reason, several violent clashes were avoided amongst the opposing factions.

In the early 1980s, joint funding of several rangers' posts was achieved with three water authorities (now companies), North West Water, Severn Trent Water and Yorkshire Water. These partnerships have proved most successful and remain in place today.

In 1984, the next Chief Ranger, Ken Drabble, began to increase the environmental education role, introducing guided walks and improving links with schools. He expanded the Countryside Maintenance Unit to cope with an increase in practical tasks. Ken had worked in the Ranger Service since the beginning of the 1960s so had considerable experience. Before retiring in 1993, he was awarded the BEM for his services to mountain rescue.

By now, the Ranger Service had developed into a comprehensive organisation including (as well as uniformed rangers) a Countryside Maintenance Team, Footpaths Officer, Pennine Way Team, Environmental Education Ranger, and Administration Support Staff. A full-time Volunteers Organiser managed the Peak Park Countryside Volunteers. This group, generally known as the PPCV, comprises people who enjoy working on physical tasks such as, footpath repairs, stone walling, tree planting, pond clearing and a host of other allied work.

The latest major changes came following appointment of the present Chief Ranger, Sean Prendergast. A new corporate image was created. Uniforms of red and grey were introduced to give a more pronounced profile. Part-time rangers were freely supplied with some protective garments of the uniform. Leasing (instead of buying) the Ranger Service vehicles, cut costs. The silver coloured Land Rovers with a livery of red lettering made the Ranger Service easily distinguishable amongst other countryside Ranger/Warden Services working in the National Park.

Three rangers became Senior Rangers, each with a special responsibility. The areas were Communications and Logistics, Training, and Health and Safety. A new training system was introduced. Computers increased the scope of the Ranger Service, with many aspects of the National Park, such as rights-of-way network, archaeology, and historical features now available on a database. Communications systems have improved with facsimile and e-mail transmissions throughout the regions. A modern high-band radio system was purchased to improve communication throughout the Park.

In order to foster goodwill and develop liaison, contact was increased with some National Parks and other protected areas abroad, especially in Poland and Slovakia. A world seminar of rangers took place in Costa Rica in 1997 through the arrangements of the International Ranger Federation. The international gathering of delegates were addressed by our Chief Ranger in a speech about the work of the Peak District National Park Ranger Service.

So, what does the future hold? In this country, despite being hugely popular, National Parks have been consistently under-funded and in recent years the financial support has, in real terms, been reduced. The visitors however do not decrease. With over 22 million visits each year, the Peak District is the most visited National Park in Europe. Indeed it is the second busiest National Park in the world (Mount Fuji in Japan is the first). There are also 38,000 people living within the National Park boundary. Their interests and concerns need just as much consideration and support as do those of the visitors.

Modern technology will probably improve communications in the Ranger Service even further and the more intensive training system should result in better qualified rangers. But the core duty of the rangers - to give protection to the National Park, especially by helping and advising the public - will no doubt continue just as it has done since those early days. However, the rangers today are very conscious of personal freedoms. The national park offers much scope for challenge and for adventure and whilst advice is willingly given when asked for, rangers do not want to become 'National Park nannies'. Training now includes plenty of information on when *not* to give advice.

As it seems everybody wants to use the National Park for their own particular function or interest, conflict will always be a problem. It is often only after becoming rangers that many people realise the almost irreconcilable difficulties that face the National Parks. Compromise is often the only solution - and even compromise can only be sanctioned if it doesn't spoil what must be saved and cherished for future generations. Because of the immense variety of tasks, it still remains difficult to pinpoint all the duties involved in the ranger's role. Suffice to say that whatever happens in the Peak District National Park it is most likely that a ranger is involved somewhere along the line.

Anybody who would like to become a volunteer ranger is always made welcome. There is an interview and a training course - but fortunately, nobody now has to match Tom Tomlinson's walking speed to the top of Kinder Scout.

Geoff Frost
Area Ranger

IT SOUNDS IDYLLIC BUT...

Rangers on the Park

There are not many areas in Greater Manchester where people have been killed in snow avalanches or become lost in blizzards. I work in one such area.

Being a ranger on the Oldham fringe of the Peak National Park has many pros and cons. The cottage that comes with the job is situated in a remote spot with a pinewood at the rear and a superb view of hills, crags and reservoirs at the front. It sounds idyllic and it is apart from a few things. During the summer, biting midges prevent any evening relaxation in the garden and all windows have to be kept shut. In winter the private road to the cottage can become impassable with snow and the overhead electricity supply occasionally fails.

Living on site also means twenty-four hour commitment. It is really more of a way of life than a job. The down side is being pestered at home when off-duty or on holiday. I was once woken-up by a young camper knocking on the door at one-thirty in the morning. He had been attacked by some ruffians who had stolen some of his camping gear. The benefits though far outweigh the problems. Being able to step outside and be immediately at work without any travelling or traffic jams to contend with is just wonderful. And of course there is the beauty of the countryside itself.

It is an odd sort of place. The nearby Saddleworth moors, made infamous by Ian Brady and Myra Hindley, have some of the wildest and loneliest countryside in the National Park. Yet after a drive of only half an hour I can be in the middle of Manchester. It is this closeness to the urban conurbation that makes the job somewhat different. For instance, unlike the Lake District with its boarding houses and hotels, it is mostly day-trippers that visit my area. They come in the thousands, especially at weekends. To the relief of the ramblers, rock-climbers and no doubt the wildlife, most of the visitors just want to picnic or take a short walk. North West Water have provided a surfaced track around one of the reservoirs allowing for access for the wheelchairs and push trolleys, which means that most sections of the public can enjoy the area and not just those who are physically fit. Of course easy access also means that the less likeable visitors are able to pursue their anti-social activities.

It's surprising what speeds can be obtained on a bicycle along the reservoir track. It usually depends on how many people are blocking the way but this often acts as a challenge to many of the Lycra clad lunatics. Some of them seem to view walkers as skittles and I am forever amazed at how quick and how high elderly pedestrians can jump. Teams of volunteer and part-time rangers are on duty at weekends. They try to advise the cyclists to slow down a bit and respect other trail users but it is often a thankless task.

Drug dealing is known to occur at the main car park and sex perverts ply their trade at the picnic site toilets at various times of the day. We try to disturb their activities as much as possible, usually by frequent patrolling and making our presence known - there's not a lot else we can do. The cleaner is best, she bangs on the doors and shouts, "Come out you dirty devils, I know what you're doing". The police have regular patrols and mount the occasional purge. A local sergeant once went undercover and dressed up as a mountain biker complete with tight shorts and a pink T-shirt. It was quite a successful ruse if you can call it that.

In dry, warm weather fire is a constant hazard especially on the high moors. We post warning notices around various points of access to ask the public to take care but in this area it can have the opposite effect. When some of the Neanderthal types see a fire-warning notice they light a fire to see if it really is possible. More than often though the problems come from youngsters camping in the woods, they just don't realise how easily a fire can spread. It is also the warm weather when gangs of youths dive off some high rocks at the water's edge and swim in the reservoir. We counted over a hundred and fifty people in the reservoir on one particular hot day. Yes there have been people drowned and they're not supposed to be in the water but how can you stop them? Even the police give up on that problem.

There is vandalism but it seems to have decreased dramatically in the last year or so. Perhaps people are becoming more caring at last. The 1980s were the worst. Hardly a month went by without signposts being smashed, stiles broken, graffiti sprayed on

rocks and gangs of foul-mouthed youths roaming about intimidating people. A murder victim was once buried in a shallow grave at the picnic site and a woman was tied to a tree and raped at the same place. This is an aspect of the job that the public doesn't often consider. They see a ranger driving about in a Land Rover or walking on the moors and think it's an easy, escapist type of job. Don't apply for a ranger's job if you want to get away from it all.

Fortunately most of the visitors are just ordinary, decent folk who are a pleasure to help and advise. It's remarkable though how many of the modern city-bred children and teenagers are unsure of themselves in the alien, countryside environment. I once watched five skinheads in the woods at the rear of the cottage. They were crouched down, moving slowly through the undergrowth in a sort of Rambo style. An old ewe happened to be grazing amongst the trees and poked her head out to see what was happening. She obviously startled the group. The leader threw up his arms, gave a sudden yell of 'SHEEP' and the intrepid warriors fled as if the devil himself had been sighted.

It is of course possible to get away from it all at times. On the high ground peace and solitude prevail. There is nowhere quite like the moors. They may be bleak and lack the scenic grandeur of great mountains but there is something special about them, something even spiritual. A lone patrol with the tang of the heather in the air and the melancholy wail of a plover in the background is a delight. Peregrine falcons nest on certain crags. At times they can be seen plummeting like free falling stones to snatch their prey from the sky. OK, so there is no payment for overtime but I don't care.

The Goyt Valley is stunning, full of contrasts with reservoirs that become mirrors on calm days and black, boiling cauldrons with white horses skimming the surface during winter's storms. There are impenetrable conifer plantations, ancient oak and beech woodlands, all changing through the seasons; myriad shades of green, brown, orange, purple and red; high moorlands of heather and bilberry. Secret places seem wild and

lonely, though rarely empty. We share them with the grouse, the deer, the skylarks and the sheep. But - the peace and quiet of the countryside? I dread sunny summer weekends.

On hot summer Sundays the heart of the valley heaves with people. I like to see the families enjoying the place, getting out into the countryside away from the shops, the neighbours and the television. Though not the traffic.

But then there are the ones I would rather not see, the dickheads. They arrive with carrier bags full of lager and a towel - diving into the reservoir off the bridge or the edge of the old quarry, mindless of the fact that it may be the last thing they ever do. The shock of the cold water can kill, so can the rocks below the surface. We tell them. They stop. We move on, they start again. What can you do? One Sunday there were two groups, about sixty of them altogether, giving each other some stick. It got ugly so we called the police. Let them try and sort it out. There is not much they can do either. The following day I go round with a bag and clear the litter. There is always litter to clear. Why can't people take it away with them?

Then there are the raves. Hundreds of people arriving in the middle of the night, with some secretive organiser making a fast buck with total disregard for the mess, damage and irritation that results. Petrol engined generators drive powerful sound systems and strobe lights. The first I know of it is a phone call from the police at midnight. They try to cope with an impossible situation - ten policemen off the street, and hundreds of idiots full of drugs and booze, throwing rocks and bottles at the police, who have to withdraw for their own safety.

We cope with the aftermath, the rubbish and the vandalism. We make plans to stop it happening again, blocking access for their vans and so on, but it costs a fortune.

Millers Dale is wonderful. The quarry is my favourite place in the whole of the Peak District. There are just so many plants and all sorts in there. Just so much; it is lovely. I prefer the White Peak to the moors. They are OK if you are in a group, especially on a good day such as in winter, when it's all blue skies and snow. But I don't like the feeling of responsibility when you're alone up on Kinder say; it is very daunting. No, I much prefer the White Peak.

There's no one part of the job that I prefer, I like it all, except for those things requiring manual strength, like mountain rescue. I'm not very big. Mind you, I enjoy crag work. I was one of those that weeded the limekilns at Millers Dale. Vegetation had taken hold everywhere so we went down on ropes with saws, spades, trowels and whatever all tied to our belts and set about clearing it. We had a laugh at one point. We had reached the third ledge which is narrower than the others and I got hopelessly jammed by my spade. So there I am, stuck fast half way down the limekilns, when an elderly couple come along. She turns to him and says in a really crabby voice, "There you are. Don't you complain next time you have to do our rockery; just be glad you don't have something as big as that to do."

I grew up on the outskirts of Oldham, and almost every weekend between the ages of 13 and 17 I was out walking or climbing or something, mainly in the Peak District, and that feeling for the area has never left me. Now I work as a ranger up in the Northern most bits of the Park. I am just a straightforward ranger and work across two areas with two Area Rangers. My job is essentially the same as the Area Ranger except that they have more autonomy and we generally do as we are asked. I work two weeks with one Area Ranger on Saddleworth Moor, and two weeks with another in Longendale. Both are very similar environments, set amongst the moorlands of the Peak District. It is bleak and inhospitable, I love its wilderness and ruggedness. You can escape everything that is artificial up there, anything that is manufactured. It's a feeling that you can only get if you are alone, if you were up there with a group you'd get a feel for what it is, but to be alone up there is something very special.

During the week it is very quiet, you might not see anybody at all. The Pennine Way crosses the high ground and we have a few walkers on that, but it's mainly in the valleys near the reservoir where most people congregate. We also have some odd ones asking where the Moors Murders took place. Some people even bring metal detectors and divining rods to look for the child's body that is still buried up there.

I appreciate that I am in a fortunate position to love my job. When people ask me how I am or how's the job, I reply 'Well, it beats working.' I have no doubts at all about my future career. When I first started in this, I did an MA in Recreational Studies, thinking I would get a ranger job and then steadily move up the ladder. As I now know the job, I no longer want to move up the ladder, I'm very happy where I am. I get asked enviously 'How do you get a job like yours?' many times every week. Well, I'm keeping hold of it.

The only thing that really frightens me is the weather. We once had to help in searching the moors on Kinder Scout because some lads were missing. There was a severe storm at the time. The rain was pelting down and thunderclaps echoed across the land. Suddenly, a particularly lengthy and bright lightening flash lit up the sky. At this time, I was on the highest point of the moor. My radio aerial, sticking out of my rucksack, began to hum with the electricity in the air. It made me realise that I was the highest thing around. Not wishing to become a burnt cinder I quickly retreated to a lower position and huddled against the side of a hillock. Somebody had to search that moor but I thought it could wait for a little while longer.

In my mind nothing beats walking up Grindsbrook to Kinder in the winter snow. The view is beautiful. In summer the walk down Lathkill Dale beside the babbling river would take some beating. Often after we had shut the hostel, I would wander up on to the moor around Druid Stone. That is my favourite spot in the whole of the Peak District. I love that moor. It has all sorts of wonderful soft memories. There is a lovely view because it is high enough to see over the ridge of Lose Hill, Back Tor etc. You can see all over. My family know to spread my ashes there. But it will be a navigation job because there are two stones, and I know which one I want to be at. If they get it

wrong, I can imagine my ashes scrabbling themselves across the moor to the right one, because they will know where they should be.

Winter is the time for heather burning. The gamekeepers burn the old heather plants in a patchwork pattern to allow fresh young plants to grow, which the red grouse feed on. It can only be done when the conditions are just right, when the heather is dry enough to burn, yet the ground is wet enough to prevent the fire from burning down into the peat below the vegetation. You can get so hot controlling the flames that you would believe you were in the devil's boiler room. And there's the smoke. If you can read the wind correctly it blows away from you, otherwise you are engulfed. Usually I finish up black and smell like bonfire night for days.

Heather burning is nothing to do with us really, but I help out the gamekeepers. It makes for a very good working relationship. Good working relationships are the crux of doing the job successfully in my area. There are so many people we need to work with. Wildlife wardens, foresters and area managers from North West Water, who actually pay half my wages and from Forest Enterprise, both of whom have large land ownerships. Ecologists, archaeologists, land agents, farmers, schools, local councils and conservation organisations. We are the first point of contact, the link, the eyes and ears of the National Park. The downside of maintaining all this liaison is that it necessitates a lot of meetings. Some weeks I seem to do nothing but go from one meeting to another. It's not what people imagine rangers doing, I'm sure. Still that's the way the job's going now. We are becoming resource managers, facilitators and advisors.

THE FIRST TIME I MET KEN DRABBLE

Rangers Starting Out

I was young and impressionable when I had my first encounter with a Peak Park Warden. I and two friends had recently been given the locations of several aircraft wrecks on Kinder Scout. Kinder and Bleaklow were little visited, except by individuals or groups trying to prove something to someone, or mad walkers. So one weekend we decided to cross from Alport to Hayfield via Doctors Gate and a trig point firstly, to complete the route and, secondly, attempt to identify certain wreck sites.

It was as thick as a bag on the tops and not a soul had been seen since the dale. Walking on a compass bearing from Doctors Gate and moving in slow mode ensuring short distance accuracy we were somewhat concerned. Though properly equipped it was nevertheless hairy in the poor visibility and travelling up and down peat groughs.

Out of the mist appeared a lone figure with a hearty 'How are you lads?' He stopped and spoke, asking where we were heading for. We explained, then ascertained our route and conditions before continuing.

A few hours later, nearing the trig point, or so we thought, a somewhat tired voice on our right said 'I see you made it then'. It was our same Warden. We walked towards the voice and found him at the trig point which we would otherwise have missed. It was like having a guardian angel. That was the first time I met Ken Drabble, who later became a Chief Ranger.

The next time I saw Ken was at his home. I was there with the Buxton Mountain Rescue Team to do with a film for a children's TV programme, *Magpie*, on Mountain Rescue. We set off up the Grindsbrook, not very far because of the *Magpie* vehicle which had to stay with us. They did some superficial filming of discovering a casualty and administering first aid and we then broke for lunch. We local people pulled out our 'butty box' and flask, sat on a hummock and proceeded to eat and discuss the day's events. We could not fail to notice a large cloth being laid down near the stream followed by three large wicker hampers - all for the *Magpie* team and film crew. Our interest was further enhanced when out of the baskets came wine, red and white, fresh salmon, chicken, fresh fruit and cream and a selection of petite fois.

The man I felt had the hardest job to do, and whom I admired because of the way in which he tackled it, was Tom Tomlinson, the first ranger in the country. Being the first he couldn't ask anyone how the job should be done, but he was so enthusiastic that it rubbed off on everyone he met including the four part-timers and then all the part-timers who followed. I joined the Service in September 1959. It was completely different from my normal job and when I started I was one of only four part-time rangers. I found in the early days that I was spending a large amount of time on public relations work, creating an image and talking about the National Park and what it could do for the locals.

Opposition to the Ranger Service initially came from the Ramblers' Association and from local farmers and it was our job to smooth it over. One of the first jobs carried out to try to understand what was happening was a people count on Langsett Moors. The rangers spent eight weekends patrolling and counting the number of people using the Moors for recreation and trying to anticipate problems. The Landowners were now getting cheap 'gamekeepers' and the National Park Board was getting valuable information. Of course the old gamekeepers were not very much in favour of this, thinking they were losing ground. A breakthrough came during a Foot and Mouth outbreak when rangers were used to stop ramblers going out on the Moor. The keepers now saw for themselves how the Ranger Service could help them in their jobs.

It was harder contacting the local farming community who were very anti-National Park. During some heavy snow storms, two of us took a Friday off work and helped Tom to clear snow, digging out on a farm road so that milk could be collected and the stock fed. We spent all Friday, Saturday and the morning of Sunday doing this. The farmer and his wife invited us in to the farmhouse for tea and cakes to thank us for our help. By Tuesday a bill had arrived at our headquarters at Aldern House for the tea and the cakes.

I think that without the Ranger Service there wouldn't have been a working, practical National Park, as ideas and concepts promulgated by the National Park passed through the Ranger Service to the locals on the ground. The Park needed the Rangers to enable co-operation with the local farmers and walkers.

I was keen on walking and having seen some of the ill-clad disasters who were also keen walkers I decided to try and be helpful by volunteering as a warden. This was in 1957/8 and obviously the range of specialist outdoor clothing was pretty well non-existent. Getting suitable equipment was very hard and money was short - what changes? Boots were available but not worn as a must as nowadays. It was difficult to get to places because you were dependent on public transport or your feet; so there were very few people who braved the high moors. It was very different from today's extensive strings of walkers wandering over the peat and heather.

Compared to the present day wardening was crude. We had no radios, no Mountain Rescue to call on and helicopters were way in the future. Shift started at around nine o'clock. We assembled and were off pretty quickly. We had some funny looks and comments from visitors, such as "Who are you?" and "What authority do you have?" However I was quite tall and became very good at looming over miscreants. Our uniform was an armband. Training happened occasionally but certainly not before you had done one or two patrols.

Kinder was better covered in heather and the erosion had hardly got going. There was no Pennine Way and once you were a mile out from Edale it was a surprise if you met anyone. Our main objective seemed to be stopping ill-equipped folk vanishing into the wild blue yonder. Most people had no concept of how quickly the weather could change on the top so advice was essential. The winters seemed to be far more severe in those days - blizzards aplenty and amazing cornices to lure the unwary. I was once with a friend on Kinder in a total white-out. It was like flying in a cloud and we quickly became disorientated. We carefully and slowly walked south and I suppose we both prayed. But it's all too easy to get lost.

My very first duty was on Kinder, the first time with my nice new badge on and I was thrown in at the deep end. On my way up Grindsbrook, I came upon this large school party. You could tell they were not used to what they were doing; the three teachers each had one of those bright orange, soft, floppy sacks; the sort that just droop everywhere. So I just followed them at a distance. One lad got separated from the others looking for gold in the stream. Finally, I caught them up right on the edge. There was one lad busy filling and refilling a kettle in the stream, trying to get some water without peat in it. "Sir is going to make us a cup of tea, but I don't fancy it with all these bits in." "And how's Sir going to make this tea?" "Oh, he's lighting a fire." So there was I on my first duty, with an ill-equipped school party, in early December, having to explain to the teacher that apart from the byelaws, lighting an open fire on peat was liable to cause a problem. He had no idea. And that tea was his sole provision for the party's drink for the whole day. He had even carried sticks and firewood all the way up to make his fire. Poor little blighters. They were already exhausted. They had come up from the south on the train the day before. Then they had been marched to the youth hostel, and now they were heading out for a long day on Kinder. I had no radio to advise other rangers to keep an eye out for them, so I did what I could. I think the full-timer went round to the hostel that evening and had a friendly chat with the teachers.

Most weekends Mum and Dad would bring me and Jono my brother out into Derbyshire. Funny but then I didn't know it was the Peak Park, everyone in Nottingham says 'we're going to Derbyshire' and folk know where you mean.

We spent a lot of time staying in the Climbing Hut under Froggatt Edge and when I was old enough I used to come out here on the Transpeak bus to Bakewell. When the weather was good I would go through Chatsworth to Froggatt and hitch if it was raining (but tell Mum I had walked). I was a sixteen year old girl and feeling very grown up and worldly-wise, you know what it's like. I met my first ranger about that time. I was camping at the bottom of a crag and he moved me on. I never thought I would be working with them then and I haven't ever dare ask him if he can remember me.

The place I still enjoy is connected to those times. You walk up through the woods from the hut, it's always wet and green with a familiar damp moss smell. I recognise some of the boulders and one very large one you have to climb over always reminds me of my mum because one of us would have to go back to her cries of 'Wait! come and get me'.

Before long you're on the top of Froggatt Edge. A stream runs through a spot I have always wanted to pitch my tent. I better not now. That would be embarrassing - to be moved on by a colleague. There's a large flat rock on a risen area of land to sit on as you look across the valley in front of you.

White Edge is behind and to the south the edge rises and then falls away into the distance. It's one of those places I can sit and look for a very long time, and remember the people I have shared this place with. Climbing times, sunny evenings losing your knuckles, 21st birthday hangovers and girlie chats, kite flying in gushing winds, scary belaying times with boyfriends insisting on climbing to the limit. One time we set off for a holiday in France and ended up here.

I had my first job away from home in the Lakes when I was seventeen leading outdoor activities for people with learning difficulties. That was the start and the next seven years I spent climbing, canoeing, doing caving centre work, working in a bar, partying and dying my hair strange colours, trying at all costs to avoid paying campsite fees and being quite roughty-toughty for a girl. I think it made a good apprenticeship for joining the Ranger Service.

In 1972 I joined up as a volunteer and then a part-timer. I was a classic part-time patrol ranger, on rota and working one shift in four. I was at Dove Stone for eight years and then two years at Crowden but then I packed it in for a while. It was a combination of things. My family commitments had increased. I had daughters who had got to the age where they needed ferrying around and combining that with the very long round trip to do my patrol duty was becoming increasingly difficult. But it was also a period of expansion in the Service which created some disatisfaction. The Service went through a period of change; full-time staff were increased, a career structure was developed for them and part-timers did not feel included. Consequently, I was getting less and less satisfaction. It wasn't like it used to be so I stopped. When I retired, I moved to Derbyshire, re-did the training and now work as a volunteer.

Things have changed. Twenty years ago your knowledge of the Park and of the Ranger Service was confined to where you worked. You tended to be part of your shift, part of your area. Dove Stone and Langsett, where I had worked, might as well have been Iceland. People never came over the hills. Nowadays the Service is much more integrated. We have role playing days on our training programmes and people are pulled in more to help with that as well as other things. Rangers do more than they used to, more countryside maintenance, more work with school, greater interaction with the public. People work across the Park. So there isn't the them-and-us situation that there used to be. It doesn't feel that volunteers are just being used as patrol-fodder for the Service. There is a nominal payment. They started paying staff to get the commitment so that they would turn out. Pay is a token gesture, a thank you for the commitment.

I was the first non-military Chief Ranger but I wasn't actually a ranger and I felt like a great, big fraud. I got the job because I'm good at fighting, good at turning bureaucracy to our advantage, at getting the resources necessary to do the job and in that I was a man for the times.

I deliberately set out to make changes. All the National Parks, not just the Peak Park had been cosseted, protected from the budget slashing that was affecting local authorities, schools, health services. When the Ranger Service was formed in 1974 it was a ground breaking move, the Service was no longer just about access agreements but became a Service that went right across the Park. However, over the years they had taken their eye off the ball and the Ranger Service model was seen as dated. There was a move away

from Ranger Sevices to Projects Officers. I knew the model wasn't dated and our job was to demonstrate that it was the best way forward. Lots of people don't know what the Peak National Park does but everyone knows what the Ranger Service is. It's the visible part of the Service. It's also a two way conduit, not just feeding down the requirements of the Peak Park but, by being part of the community, feeds back up to the decision makers. I could see the latent potential here but there were factors not being stimulated. I wanted the Service to be at the cutting edge again, go further, try new things.

From my experience in local authority I knew the storm was coming in, that from now on we would need to continually justify our existence, our funding. Every one of my predecessors thought the rangers were brilliant but couldn't quantify what it was that made us special. We needed to quantify and demonstrate that in a new language which related to the changes taking place in the outside world, or else the world would move on by and we would be left behind, weakened and vulnerable. Special pleading had meant that there had only been intermittent cuts but I knew that wouldn't work anymore.

We had to promote and re-define the package. We re-invented ourselves as an authoritative, not authoritarian body, that people could approach. The 1995 legislation had better focussed what we had to do as a National Park - conserve and enhance the beauty of the Park, promote opportunities for enjoyment and understanding of its special qualities and have awareness of the local communities. This legislation did not come with extra resources. We have had a 20% cut in real terms over the last three years. During that time we've expanded the radio frequency, changed the Land Rovers, changed uniform and expanded uniform provision. We've expanded the Environmental Programme, the role of conservation volunteers, the Training programme and its resources. We've made links with Losehill Hall - the National Park Study Centre - and work with archaeology and environmental services. We now generate far more of our own income through partnership and European funding but we're not even halfway there. Perhaps there isn't a 'there' that we can arrive at - there will always be something we can strive for, something we can improve, but we do have the potential to get back to the cutting edge.

ALL MAPS AND ARGUMENTS
Rangers and Locals

Before I became a Ranger I had a very similar type of job which gave me a good grounding. I was a Rights-of-way Officer, dealing with footpaths and bridleways, an extremely contentious job. A mate of mine reckons that the motto of that job should be whatever is Latin for 'All maps and arguments'.

You have to adopt a middle line on that job between farmers and walkers. It's all intricate and involved, it's a legal situation above all else. It could be quite tricky and insulting. I had one farmer who had a legally recognised footpath running through his farmyard, but he had been obstructing it for years. It was our job to lean on him, and he was continually haranguing and bothering us, so we sent him a letter, which is what we were supposed to do, outlining the legal case for the footpath and that he'd better let people pass or we'd take him to court.

He was an elderly man and he took ill and was rushed to hospital. His wife rang me up and said he was in intensive care and that if he died it was my fault. This was very upsetting to me, not just that the guy was very ill, but that I had upset his wife so much. Thankfully he didn't die.

That kind of experience though was very useful for when I became a ranger. In this job we are faced with awkward farmers and awkward ramblers. It is fair to say that the majority of farmers aren't enthusiastic about recreationalists. I had a farmer who had his barn burnt down. There was no real suggestion of arson but when the question was asked if this farmer had any enemies, everyone fell about laughing. He wasn't a popular fella. However, on that same farmer's land, some people who had just bought a new 4x4, opened up his gate, drove into his fields and thought they'd try them out, digging up his land.

In many ways, our main road in this job is to educate each to the other's ways.

One rambler's group complained that I had erected a 'private land' sign on some moorland. They were quite correct, I had done this following a request from the farmer and the land was indeed private. The sign was only six inches by three inches and dark brown in colour. They called me a landowners' lackey and many other names in a similar vein. They even had a newspaper take pictures of the sign. This was done with a wide-angled lens close to the sign with a rambler stood in the background. It appeared as if the sign was huge - I learnt then how easily newspapers can distort the truth. These particular ramblers then intimated as I was a public servant I shouldn't have erected the sign. What they failed to realise was that the farmer was also a member of the public. The sign is still in place, ten years after the event.

Overall, my direct experience of rangers has been quite limited, but at times they have been very helpful and useful to me; such as keeping an eye on the perimeter of my land where it abuts against the Monsal Trail. They have let me know about broken fences and stock getting out. They also keep a check on the footpaths and keep stiles and such like in good order. They've also brought injured stock to my attention.

But I have to say that footpaths and walkers are not a problem to me. Most folk, the general walkers so to speak, are OK. Some aren't so good at map reading and get themselves lost occasionally. They see a gate, go through and get a bit wrong and perhaps end up climbing over where they shouldn't, but it's never done deliberate. The only gripe I've had is with the 'ramblers'. I have one particular path which cuts across the corner of a field to the stile, and it's a field I crop. The ranger down at Millers Dale was very helpful and had some wooden signs made up saying, 'Please walk by the wall side', which everyone did, instead of going through the crop. But the ramblers wouldn't. They insisted on taking the direct line, and I suppose they were strictly correct in a legal sense, but it was only another ten yards or so and there was no real need to be so dogmatic.

I was glad to be with big Dave the day we met a really nasty bloke. We had to check out the route of a footpath. It was a rarely used path and was somewhat overgrown. It skirted around the front of a large house then crossed several fields below. We had our

maps out and were checking the line with compasses when this man and woman came out of the house. The man began shouting at us. "What the hell do you think you're doing on my land?"

We introduced ourselves and politely informed him that we were checking the line of the public footpath. He began arguing that the path didn't exist and nobody ever used it. Fortunately I had the definitive map and the footpath was clearly marked.

"I don't give a bugger what the map says, get off my land," he bellowed. The woman, whom we presumed was his wife, kept nodding her head at everything he said. She then told us he was a local councillor so we had better be careful. In some ways, it was quite funny. There was one point though where I thought he was going to thump me. I needn't have worried. Dave stepped forward and glowered at him. Never said a word. Just stood in front of him and stared. The man soon backed down.

It was all settled through official channels at the head office. The man had to admit that the footpath was a public right-of-way. But that wasn't the end of it. He made sure that walkers didn't stray off the correct route by painting the tops of every stile in bright pink. He's dead now but I always think about him when I walk that footpath. I just hope there is no such thing as ghosts.

I was talking to a gamekeeper who thought the rangers did a reasonable job but felt that more rangers were needed on the hills. There were too many people trespassing. He was glad of our assistance in helping him deal with a hang-glider last year (who had landed in the middle of his best heather during nesting time) but considered we should have more powers. In the incident with the hang-glider, all we did in the end was give advice. (I think he thought that we should have been able to at least castrate the hang-glider and suspend his wings from the nearest tree).

"There's no point in advising folk if they take no damned notice. Because what do you do then? Nothing. Absolutely bloody nothing. You should be prosecuting more of them - arrest 'em if need be. Take these mountain bikers - they're all over the moors

these days. They're a pain in the arse. They do what they want and nobody does anything about it. The Peak Park should be stopping them."

I explained that we did advise mountain bikers whenever we came across them on the open moor. Indeed mountain biking was now an offence under the new bye-laws on Access Land. However, as his moor was private there was little the rangers could do except give advice. And wasn't giving advice a better thing anyway? Educating the public and all that?

"Education's all right but it's not enough. You've got to be firm with them. These people need dealing with. The trouble with a lot of you rangers is you spend too much time telling folk where they can go instead of where they can't. Do y' know what I mean?" I nodded, there was no way I was going to disagree - I have to work with this guy.

MR AND MRS BLOODY MIDDLE CLASS
Rangers and Visitors

The worst thing about dealing with the public is not knowing how they will react. Sure we receive training about the best way to approach and how to handle aggression, but it's the uncertainty that's the worrying thing. Sometimes you feel really happy and everything seems well in the world, then you come across a problem. Take a simple thing like a dog off its lead running about near sheep. No matter how often you've dealt with that situation (and it's usually hundreds of times) you still don't know how the dog's owner is going to react.

It's not always the rough looking people that are the worst, far from it. Give me a yob any day, at least their behaviour is usually true to form and when it's not - well it's a pleasant surprise. No, it's the arrogant ones that really get on my nerves. Mr and Mrs Bloody Middle Class that think they are a cut above everyone else. Some of them treat you like dirt because they know you're a public servant and can only argue to a point. And if they have children with them - stand well back. It's almost as if they want to show their kids that nobody will ever be allowed to tell mummy or daddy what's right or wrong. Thankfully they're in the minority; most visitors are great and very understanding.

Rangers need to have a love of the countryside and the ability to deal with people in a diplomatic way. I think the major part of the job is to protect the countryside. I wouldn't be attracted to the job myself but I regularly help my husband by answering the phone and dealing with numerous enquiries.

We live in a cottage provided by the National Park Authority. This is on site in the area so there are always people knocking on the door and asking for advice. I don't mind this as I rather have them ask instead of doing something wrong. The worst time though is at lambing time when walkers bring us young lambs they have 'found' on the moor. They don't realise the trouble this causes for the farmer. The sheep around here often become trapped in the water channels, usually after being chased by dogs - this is the most frequent thing we have to answer callers about.

Most people are appreciative and grateful for any help but there have been occasions when they just think we live here for their convenience. The worst case was when a teenage boy drowned whilst crossing a flooded stream. He was a member of a group from an outdoor pursuits centre. It was a dreadful evening with heavy rain and gale force winds. My husband was out at the scene meeting the police diving unit. I had seven of the other teenagers in the house; I comforted them, made them hot drinks, gave them something to eat and lent them some dry clothes. I never saw the clothes again.

On another occasion a really rough looking woman called at the house. She was pushing a buggy-chair in which sat a dirty-faced kid with a dummy stuck in his mouth. She said her boyfriend had walked off after having a row with her and she couldn't find him. My husband was off-duty at the time and we were in the middle of our evening meal. I said he would come out and help her to search for her boyfriend as soon as he had finished his dinner. The woman was really indignant, she said, "Oh don't 'effin' bother if he can't come right now, let him finish his bloody dinner instead."

There had been severe snowfalls and the A628 was blocked with drifts of over five feet deep in places. The police had closed the road and we were patrolling in case of any stranded motorists. A Volvo which had ignored the warning signs trundled up the road heading towards the high ground. We stopped the car and advised the driver, an arrogant, middle-aged man. He refused to turn around and stated we needn't worry as his car had been fitted with snow tyres. We found him later - his car half buried in a snowdrift. He was a much humbler man than before.

The mountain biker had ridden across the moors along the Pennine Way. We were ready to stop and advise him about cycling on what is in effect a footpath. As we approached him he turned to avoid us and his front wheel slipped into a boggy section. The bike stopped instantly and he tumbled over the handlebars into stinking, black peat. We didn't bother with the advice.

One weird guy who was from some obscure religious group stated that the followers of his religion had to be baptised in natural waters. He requested permission to use Yeoman Hey reservoir for this purpose, adding that there would be about sixty people involved, wearing white robes. I told him that he would need to contact the water authority manager and added that I didn't think there was much chance of his request being granted. The man stared at me, wide-eyed and said, "Why not? Is the manager an atheist?"

Some dreamy environmental group had hung a variety of metal chimes with poetry attached to them from the trees in a picnic site. They left a notice explaining that it had been done as an experiment of peace and tranquillity. There was also a pencil and notebook requesting anyone passing to give their comments. The entries (those printable) were as follows:

* You lot are ninety-pence short of a pound.
* Leave only footprints in the countryside.
* Shift your junk, don't litter our countryside with it.
* Litter louts - keep your thoughts to yourselves.
* It saddens me that bearded, green cretins have invaded our countryside.
* You have two days to remove this lot - otherwise it will be removed for you - Signed: National Park Ranger.

Stanton Moor is a fascinating part of my area. Its history stretches back thousands of years and there are a lot of ancient remains including Nine Ladies stone circle. The moor is privately owned, but subject to a management agreement with the National Park, so I am involved with the site quite a lot. During the summer solstice the site takes on a special significance, a bit like Stonehenge, and there can be two hundred or so people gathered at the stone circle, illegally I might add. But as long as they're not doing any damage then they're tolerated. I go up and talk to them, to get the message across that

the site shouldn't be damaged in any way. There's not a lot we could do to shift them anyway.

The site has been used for thousands of years and this is really only another cultural use.

There are some sights to be seen up there though, with jugglers, music, campfires and dogs running round, it's like a medieval fair.

One year we had to call in a Mountain Rescue team to carry off a half-naked young woman who had been drinking and who knows what else. She had been dancing from stone to stone and had fallen off and broken her leg. This year at the solstice it rained solidly for three days. I wasn't unduly upset. It made things pleasantly quiet for a change.

There aren't many strange characters in my area, my colleague has most of those but his area is in Staffordshire so enough said. There is one elderly chap though who is a gem. He lives in a tumbledown barn with half a roof. I believe he actually sleeps under the section that is open to the sky. Despite being odd he's very clever and can relate masses of information about astronomy. Indeed when I had to question him about a problem with a stile he spent the first ten minutes talking about the planets. The thing is - he doesn't talk directly to you face to face; he turns to one side as if chatting to an invisible person. It's a bit disconcerting at times - addressing an ear.

One of the most memorable experiences is meeting the bloke that walks on Black Hill with no clothes on. He's a frightening fella. He just walks about with a little rucksack and pink socks and that's it. Sheila was a bit shocked when she saw him so he started wearing shorts after that. He used to say it was bracing, but we said, "No thanks."

A THING ABOUT DOGS
Rangers and Animals

The height of farm gates is determined, not so much to prevent animals escaping, but for the optimum position in which a person can comfortably rest their elbows on the top rail. Leaning on gates is a popular countryside pastime. It is something that is enjoyed by all sorts of people, from farmers chatting about livestock prices to tourists admiring some distant view. Rangers have a liking for leaning on gates owing to their inquisitive nature (and not as some less kindly folk would say because they are all nosy buggers).

It was a miserable, drizzly day that found Gordon and myself leaning on the gate overlooking Fred Skinner's farmyard. At the far end of the yard, steam rose from a flock of noisy sheep that were penned inside an enclosure. In the foreground, walking freely about amongst the puddles, were several chickens, a strutting cock, and a gander, which was known by the name of Tyson.

To the side of the gate was a stile and next to the stile was a signpost pointing the direction of a public footpath across the farmyard. It was here that two walkers, a young man and woman each with a surprisingly aloof disposition, clambered over the stile and began to make their way across the farmyard. Normally we would have warned them. However, as they had ignored our greeting of good morning and had given us a look as if they had just trodden in something nasty, we decided to say nothing.

They sauntered along laughing and deliberately frightening the chickens and the cock causing them to scatter in a crescendo of cackles and feather shaking flurries. The man, of whom we had now decided was a couple of rocks short of a boulder, began waving his arms and making bleating noises imitating the sounds of the sheep. This brought squeals of girlish laughter from the woman who probably thought he was a real Jack-the-lad.

During this time, Tyson had waddled to the far end of the yard and was hidden from view behind the sheep enclosure – an ambush position he had learned to be most profitable in previous confrontations. As the walkers drew level, he launched his attack. This came in a series of gabbles, hisses, and pecking motions of such rapidity that any ordinary goose would have suffered a severe headache. The walkers dashed in a panic towards the next stile, the woman holding her bottom and the man also holding something of a personal nature. As he ran, he was shouting something about a duck in hell. This was strange because there wasn't a duck to be seen anywhere.

This noisy encounter had alerted Fred Skinner who soon shooed Tyson away with a few curses and several kicks that had no hope of connecting. The walkers, now safe on the other side of the stile, were bellowing that the footpath was a right-of-way and such aggressive creatures shouldn't be allowed to wander about the farmyard.

"Ah well, best go and have a word with Fred," said Gordon, stretching as he eased away from the gate.

"Yes," I replied, noting the location of Tyson. "You first."

It was Sunday 26 November 1995 and the day started normally enough. We turned up at Parsley Hay and sat down for a coffee and briefing. John asked if he could patrol around the Alstonefield area, we all agreed and he went off. After ten minutes John came through on the radio, saying he needed assistance in Hide Lane, Hartington as there was a wallaby in the road. We asked him to repeat his message. Sure enough he said, "I have a wallaby in the road near to Hartington". I jumped into the Land Rover with a large shovel and half a dozen bin bags and arrived to find John standing on one side of the road with a number of visitors and right opposite was a real, living wallaby. I contacted Andy, "John's not on drugs, there is a real wallaby here, get some help". After about half an hour Andy turned up with Geoff Howe, to say that Staffordshire Wildlife Rescue were on the way. Another half hour went by and along came Jon Hodges and Dave from the wildlife sanctuary and, watched by quite a crowd of visitors, we proceeded to surround the animal. With great skill the wallaby was ushered towards a catch net held by Jon and Dave and within seconds was caught and put in a cage in their van. After a couple of weeks in the animal hospital he was re-released, this time at the West Midlands Safari Park.

Kinder Scout has had more than its fair share of human tragedy. Walkers have become lost, wandering about aimlessly, panicked by the ghostly hill fog that often shrouds the bleak moor. Some have fallen from great heights and suffered snapped limbs or bloody contusions. A few have paid the ultimate price and have taken their last breath amidst the wild expanse of peat bogs. Cries for help are often received at the National Park Information Centre at Edale. It was following such a plea that rangers and a Mountain Rescue team found themselves struggling up snow-encrusted slopes to help a heart attack victim. Conditions were severe and the rocks were covered in thick ice.

This was no ordinary rescue. For instance, it is unusual to find a casualty covered in thick, white hair from head to foot. It is also rare to find one tied to a rucksack in case they recover and run off. But then, it's not often that rangers are called out to carry off sick dogs.

An Old English Sheepdog named Henry had collapsed and his distressed owner refused to leave the dog, sending her grown-up son down to Edale to summon help. As darkness approached, she also became worried about her son (priorities now becoming clearer) and left Henry tied to a rucksack. However, help was on its way in the form of two intrepid rangers. They struggled to lift the heavy dog but even their combined strength was not enough to move him any appreciable distance. A Mountain Rescue team was duly summoned.

Henry was eventually secured to a mountain rescue stretcher with his head facing forward and his paws lolling over the edge. The docile dog then enjoyed a free ride down the wintry slopes to be reunited with his mistress at Edale. He later recovered and was last heard of trying to join the St Bernard Mountain Rescue team. We believe he quite fancied himself with a barrel of brandy tied around his neck.

We were at the top of Grindsbrook, with a party of trainees and found a long-haired dachshund wandering miles from its owner. Now it's hardly a breed renowned for sheep-worrying, but we were obliged to approach the chap, expecting problems. In the

end we had a very reasonable chat, more of a debate really; all very constructive. I produced a piece of baler twine from my bag which he put on the dog as a lead. I expect he took it off again as soon as we were out of sight.

There was one difficult occasion when one of our tenant farmers rang me in the office, mid-week, and asked me to contact the police. He had found a big alsatian having a go at his sheep and he had shot it. In the situation as he described it, he was quite within his rights, but the owner eventually turned up and got very irate. Unfortunately, he then had a heart attack and died; very difficult.

A ranger of my acquaintance had a thing about dogs and probably still does. Whether he'd been bitten as a lad I'm not sure but they, and their owners, were seen as the enemy.

One weekend we were on patrol, up on the moor, when my colleague spotted a lone walker with a dog which was not on a lead, although it was walking close to heel. The area we were in was subject to an access agreement, that's privately owned land that the public are allowed to go onto provided they abide by the byelaws, so strictly speaking the dog should have been on a lead, though usually when they were well controlled I didn't bother. But my friend was of a different opinion and much to my dismay, we approached the man, ranger badges proudly displayed.

When we were near, but before we could speak, even to say hello, the man looked up and said "I know what you're going to say but bugger off". I smirked. My colleague didn't, but we buggered off anyway.

At my interview for the job I told a little white lie. It was down in the South of the Park and there were some railway trails, so someone thought it would be a good idea to put the ranger on a horse. So when they asked me if I could manage a horse, I lied through my teeth. Apparently 940 people had applied for only two posts, and that was in the Seventies when there were plenty of jobs around. In my defence, they hadn't directly asked me if I could actually ride a horse.

After the interview I went down to South Wales and had some riding lessons. I got the job and was dressed up with these big riding breechers, looking a right Charlie, and I was issued with a horse. It was called Mutley.

Mutley had a will of his own. He was grey and white and massive. He was sixteen and a half hands high, he looked like a cart horse. It was a battle of wills between me and him, both of us were determined not to back down. I once took my wife to see him and we climbed over the gate into the field and Mutley was high up on the hill, about two hundred yards away. I shouted 'Come on Muts' and he was off, stampeding. Charging straight at us. He liked to play this game, he would run towards me, then run round me three times and then run off. My wife wasn't hanging around for that though, she was off over the gate.

One day he chucked me off. I'd had him in the corral for the winter and decided that when spring came, I needed to take him out. He was very frisky. We were on the trail and I'd had enough and he'd had enough. I was running him at walls to try and get him to stop, I knew he wouldn't jump over them, he was too lazy. But he a ran me to an embankment, dropped his shoulder, and threw me off. I rolled for thirty feet down that embankment, but I had to keep rolling, he followed me over hoping to trample on me.

He eventually got a disease and had to be put down. He probably was made into dog food. If there is any poetic justice, then my dog would have eaten Mutley.

I DON'T NORMALLY TALK ABOUT THIS
Rangers' Side of the Story

I was once patrolling on Black Hill in severe hill fog. I reached the trig point and decided to have a cup of coffee. From some distance away I could hear raised voices arguing. Assuming the people arguing were lost, I set off across the peat haggs and eventually came across an outdoor pursuits group. They were indeed totally lost and were very glad to see a ranger. I asked them where they were heading and they said a trig point (from where I had just come from). They asked me to guide them there and I immediately agreed. Then with horror it struck me that I had no idea where I was - having reached their location by following the sound of their voices. Looking around, all I could see was a shroud of fog. "What compass bearing will you be setting?" asked their leader. "Err, not quite sure just yet," I said opening my map and flapping it about in order to gain some time. A map and compass are useless in fog if you don't know where you are. Suddenly I spotted my footprints in the peat and a flush of hope surged through me. I could follow my prints back to the trig point. "I'll not bother with the map," I said, turning to the surprised leader. From then on I darted across the haggs, turning this way and that, following my footprints until we reached the trig point. The group were astounded.

"That's amazing, I've never seen such navigation. God, you must know this moor like the back of your hand," the leader said.

"Oh...well...yes, it's just a matter of experience," I said, feeling much relieved - and very, very guilty.

I was on patrol from Crowden Briefing Centre. I was with an assistant ranger who never appeared to be properly equipped. We were picking up rubbish and so had our black plastic bags in hand. We noticed two strapping young lads in short shorts and T-shirts striding down Crowden Brook towards us when my companion decided to stop them. "Excuse me," he said, "You didn't ought to be out wearing shorts up here in this weather." "You're too late mate," one of them said, "We're just finishing the Pennine Way". I could have wished for a large hole to have opened up and swallowed me.

There is a mountain rescue stretcher called a split-Thomas. Each half can be carried on a rescuer's back just like a huge rucksack, the halves are assembled to form the full-size when the casualty is reached. I found myself carrying one of these stretcher halves up a snow covered slope to a casualty on the top of Kinder. Part of the way up I slipped and landed on my back in deep snow. Like a toppled over beetle, I couldn't get up and had to wait in this position until another rescuer found me and assisted me to my feet. I don't normally talk about this.

We received a radio call from Andy the Area Ranger asking if we had time to help get a cow out of Lathkill Dale. Thinking that chasing a loose cow around for half an hour would not do us any harm we agreed and set off. The next radio call told us the cow was dead. The truck was parked at Monyash, we walked down the valley and on meeting two ramblers we asked them if they had seen a dead cow.

"No, only a farmer with a big axe."

My stomach turned. We smelt the cow before we saw it. The animal had fallen off a cliff two days ago in the steepest part of the dale, there was no way to get the truck in.

On a slope under the cliff stood the farmer with an axe which must have been four feet long, he was chopping up the cow and putting bits of it into bags. First we tried carrying the bags up out of the dale but it was a struggle. A bag with a cow's leg in must weigh one hundredweight and the bags kept splitting open. We gave up on this idea. So next the farmer drove his tractor to the top of the cliff and used our ropes to haul the bags up. Some of them dropped off but eventually it was done. One of the guys was a vegetarian and he didn't like it much, but saying that, I'm not and I didn't like it either. We kept having to run off to get some clean air. The farmer thanked us.

I'd noticed the pile of rubbish a couple of days before. Most remote car parks are victims of fly tipping from time to time. So we returned with the trailer and started clearing up. We were heaving rubbish into the trailer, kitchen units, a bed, soggy cardboard,

disposable nappies - dirty of course, all manner of unwanted bits and pieces.

Working along the side of the car park we came to a large pile of hardboard which we started shifting. Under the pile was a wooden box about four feet long. It was covered with a plastic sheet and locked. My brain immediately jumped into overdrive and my first thought was, 'guns'. A terrorist arms cache had been discovered a few years earlier, though not here. My second thought was, 'a body'. I tried to convince myself that I was being ridiculous by picking the box up. It was too light to be guns or a body. Should we try and open it here or take it back to base? It could be cash. We should take it away with us I thought. So I started to walk away with it and it wouldn't come. Then I noticed the cable. A thick black cable ran from the box into the small patch of woodland behind the car park. We followed the cable and discovered that it went up into a tree. There sitting on a branch was a small video camera. We put two and two together and realised that it could be there as part of an undercover police operation to catch car thieves. A couple of enquiries on the radio confirmed this. Feeling a bit of a fool, I climbed the tree in a gesture of bravado and pulled a face at the camera.

Several hundred children can now be let loose in the countryside after attending our annual Countryside Safety exhibition.

It's a four day event and the opening day always begins with nervous tension. The display had been carefully arranged with posters portraying the dangers that might be found in the countryside. We had obtained several shop window dummies and dressed them in various types of clothing to highlight what is suitable and unsuitable for walking on the hills. One of the mannequins had been placed on a mountain rescue stretcher to resemble a casualty. A bandage, speckled with red ink, was tied around its forehead to add realism.

A shout of, "THEY'RE HERE" heralded the arrival of the first coach. The shout was delivered in a panicky manner like that of a fire warning. After a rumbling noise, somewhat similar to wildebeest stampeding across the Serengeti, the hall became alive

with uniformed darlings. Eager-eyed and filled with anticipation they had a minor scuffle until their teacher restored order. We divided them into manageable groups; my colleague Neil took one group to a table that had a display of footwear.

"Now then children my name is Neil and I am going to show you the sort of boots that might be dangerous when walking in the countryside." He picked up a pair that had soles like the surface of a bald tyre. His intention was to convey the safety message that good treads are needed on footwear to prevent people slipping.

"What do you think you would need on the bottom of these boots to stop you from slipping?" Neil asked.

There was a brief silence then a hand shot up and the answer came, "Yer feet."

I took a group of the children to look at the mannequins. One of them had been dressed as a rock climber. Despite being a male dummy it had curly blonde hair and one of those syrupy, inane smiles that such dummies have. It was a type that would have looked fine in the window of a transvestite tailor's shop. A placard hung around its neck with the words, ACTION MAN.

A thickset lad with the demeanour of a bare-knuckle bruiser pulled my sleeve to gain attention. He pointed to the dummy. "What's he supposed to be?"

"A rock climber," I replied, "one of the hard men."

The boy circled the dummy staring at it like one might stare at a burnt dinner. After a lengthy examination he turned to me and said, "Looks more like a poofter to me."

This annual safety exhibition forms part of our environmental awareness role and of which we receive the necessary training. However, there are many things that the training doesn't cover. Things like when the children openly scratch themselves in places that should only be scratched in private. That they make noises that are best not described but leave aromas like those emitted from some catalytic converters. They stick grubby fingers in their noses and carefully examine the result. And so it was with my group. An offensive appeared. The children giggled and looked at each other accusingly.

"It were Darren."

"No it weren't."

"Yes it were, you're always doing it."

"No I'm not you stupid cow."

I raised my hands, "That will do. Now start paying attention." I took them to the stretcher. A petite, white-faced girl couldn't take her eyes off the mannequin. She seemed intrigued with the red-stained bandage. The thickset boy bent forward to examine it. He grabbed hold of the mannequin's head and before I could stop him had twisted it off the body. This brought squeals of delight from the other children, except for the white-faced girl who instantly collapsed in a faint. Her teacher rushed forward to help her and almost tripped over the stretcher. More squeals from the children.

"I once slipped on a dead frog," said one girl.

Her friend pulled a face, "Ugh...I bet it was all slimy and horrible."

"It was, all its giblets came out."

I shook my head and looked across the room. Another colleague, Andy was trying to explain the dangers of swimming in reservoirs.

"What do you think might be dangerous in a reservoir?" He asked. A mass of hands went up and he pointed to one boy who gave the answer as jellyfish. Another lad, no doubt with a good future as an undertaker, shouted "dead bodies".

Neil had now moved on from explaining about boots and was instructing his group about the sort of clothes to wear on the moors. One mannequin had been dressed in appropriate hill-walking clothing and another one, a much shorter female mannequin, was wearing a thin blouse and shorts. Neil pointed to this one and asked, "Why do you think it would be dangerous for this woman to go walking on the moors?"

"Because her legs are too short," came the immediate answer.

At the end of the four days and after dealing with around seven hundred children, the exhibition had obviously taken its toll of the rangers. I didn't realise how badly this had been though until Andy, relaxing with a cup of coffee, mused that he thought one of the female mannequins was particularly attractive.

STILL STANDING STOUTLY
Rangers on the Job

The Pennine Way stretches from Edale to Kirk Yetholm in Scotland. Parts of the route traverse the deep peat bogs of Kinder Scout and Bleaklow. Over the years many types of footpath construction have been experimented with, some more successful than others. The problem was always the same. The peat is very deep, ten feet or so in places, and so soft and wet that most materials sink without trace fairly quickly.

One method we tried involved digging out the line of the path and installing polystyrene blocks which were about three feet square by six inches thick. The idea was that the polystyrene would float on the soft ground and also would not rot. On top of the blocks we laid a thick woven material with a couple of inches of crushed stone topping it off, providing a good surface to walk on. We did about two hundred yards up there using this technique, during the summer, the dry ground being easy to work on.

When it came time to pack up our site hut and tools, to move to a work site at a lower altitude for the winter, the weather changed quite dramatically and became very wet, very quickly. The line of the path soon became waterlogged and the polystyrene path really was floating. Through the rain clouds a lone walker appeared over the horizon and made a beeline for our new path. As he stepped on to the path an amazing thing happened. The impact of his steps on the path caused it to start moving. It began undulating like a wave. The expression on his face was a picture, a mixture of disbelief, bemusement and fear. Needless to say, that particular experiment in footpath construction was not successful and we had to re-do that section in the end.

I've been working for the Ranger Service for about three years now - I think I've lost count. I'm interested in natural history and trained for this sort of conservation work at college, we lay gritstone slabs on the Pennine Way.

Working on the Pennine Way and doing a specific job means a lot to us and to the people we're doing it for. The standard of our work has got a lot better over the years, we've learnt as we've gone along. Now we have reached the peak of our work on the moors. We know how good it should look and how it should be. The worst thing about our job is the monotony - without a shadow of a doubt. In the winter you just can't get out. There's four people in the team with loads of different skills that are just wasting away. It does your head in. A lot of the time we're just sitting there waiting for the weather to break so we can get out and weigh a bit of stone. Because we've got to walk out so far on to site you don't want to commit yourself to going out there if the weather turns really bad and we've got to come straight back. It's frustrating. We're lucky if we can get low level footpath work in the winter otherwise you tend to bicker, end up on each others' nerves.

The stone slabs are helicoptered on to the moor and we have radio communication with the pilots. Many of them are ex-army. Some are very staid and professional but others are real nut-cases. We had one last year that played a different character each time he returned from the moor - one time he came back as Fifi La Rue. He kept on about having kippers for breakfast. I think he was going stir-crazy flying back and forth 300 times. But he was a superb pilot, despite being an absolute nutter.

The best thing about the job is what we achieve with regards to wildlife. If we alter a stretch of path from seventy yards to a stone's width that means we're creating a habitat for birds. A lot of people think we do this job for walkers but that's not the reason (not my reason anyway). I can't be doing with walkers. I'm doing it for wildlife. I'd rather look out for Golden Plover than walkers. It's having something to show for it all. The path will be there in 150 years time long after I've popped me clogs. We're not under masses of pressure, though sometimes it would be nice to be.

People see us working but never really know who we are. "So you're the National Trust?", "Council?", "You must be volunteers?". One day I was asked if the lads were "naughty boys" doing community service. One man was genuinely amazed when he saw us working. He'd never seen a stile being made before, just thought that they were there in the countryside. "I suppose you're a stilest" he said.

We do meet some people. There was a stile behind the Roaches that needed replacing about a quarter of a mile from where we parked the truck. The position of the stile was a little ambiguous but we had a look at the line of the footpath on the map and were pretty sure it was OK. Two of the team went over whilst the others stayed to repair a gate. At lunch we met up, discussed the stile and were convinced it was correct.

In the distance over the heather and bilberry I could make out the figure of a woman coming towards us, not screaming or shouting or even waving but I could tell she was angry. The team saw her too and retreated to the back of the truck. As soon as she came into earshot she shouted "You've put it in the wrong place" and I got a real ear full. Most situations we can handle but this time we had to call the Area Ranger in to calm the situation. The thing I really remember was knowing she was so mad from such a way away.

Some people say everything and others nothing at all. A stone step needed repairing in a wall on a footpath in Thorpe. A busy path used by walkers to get to the Peveril of the Peak pub. The wall was higher on one side than the other and sheep were managing to jump from one pasture to the other. We had done a good job and were just off home when the farmer came over to see how we had got on. We leant on a gate admiring our work. As we engaged in general chit chat a sheep jumped over the stone step we had supposedly mended. I pretended not to notice and so did the farmer. As we carried on chatting another, then another and another sheep jumped over the step, until twelve sheep from the neighbour's farm were on the farmer's pasture.

Nothing was said about the sheep.

"Right" said the farmer. "I must be off, guess I'll be seeing you tomorrow."

I was working down in the dales on some badly eroded footpaths. We had a lot of Borstal boys with a bunch of wheelbarrows and great big pile of stones that we were going to spread on the footpaths to strengthen them. I had ordered a JCB to come down and help us lift them.

Where we had dumped the stones, there were two ancient stone columns at the entrance of some gate. The local Lord of the Manor was very proud of these columns and talked at length about them. When we got to the end of the job, I went to say goodbye to the JCB driver and watched as his digger arm swung round and broke one of these precious columns in two.

I had no idea how I could face this Lord of the Manor and tell him the news, so I didn't. In the local village there was a garage with a shop, so I bought two tubes of plastic padding, mixed it all up, laid it on the stump, got the JCB and some ropes and lifted the column back in place. We gathered some moss and glued the two pieces of stone together using the moss. The Lord of the Manor never found out and the pillar is still standing to this day.

Stone stiles are funny things. Some fall down, or are pushed, almost as soon as they are built. Others seem to last forever, defying gravity even though their foundations are undermined and great holes appear in their sides. Along with my team-mate Claire, I rebuilt an old stile in a blizzard once. It was very cold and a driving wind was blowing frozen snow horizontally across the moor. We were to build the stile in a dry-stone wall, but, as a precaution against future collapse we decide to use mortar in critical places. First we tried to clear the ground of loose stones, this could only be done with a sledgehammer, they were so firmly frozen to the ground. The old foundations had to stay as they were, they were too solid to move. Building was easy, as soon as we placed a stone on the wall it froze into position with no sign of looseness anywhere. The trouble came when we came to fix the mortar. Everything was frozen solid. We pounded the frozen lumps of sand and cement into powder with a hammer. However, our water was all ice and it turned to crystals when it was given the same treatment. So, when we mixed it all together, instead of mortar all we got was a damp powder. By now we were so cold we used the mixture anyway. We finished off the stile and packed our tools away as quickly as we could, caring more for our fingers and ears than anything

else. This was not the best stile we had ever built. Soon we were heading back to base and warmth.

It was 18 months before I passed that way again. I approached the stile with trepidation, half expecting it to be just a pile of stones. But there it was still standing stoutly as when Claire and I had built it. There was no sign of mortar, the rain had washed it away long before. Now, three years on, the stile still stands and looks set for many more years to come. As I said, stone stiles are funny things.

Parts of Staffordshire are very wet and boggy. One day two of us went to do some work to repair a stile on a footpath that crossed a field that looked OK. My friend set off with shovel in hand whilst I was still at the Land Rover. I was engrossed in whatever I was doing when a shout grabbed my attention. Looking across the field I saw my colleague had sunk up to his knees in a wet patch. It looked so funny I couldn't help laughing. My normally calm, quiet friend did not see the funny side though and began shouting that I should help him out as soon as possible. From where I was, the situation just seemed so ludicrous, and his shouting and waving just made it funnier. So I just laughed some more.

Well, the more I laughed, the more he ranted and raved, completely out of character, and the funnier it all seemed, so I laughed till I cried. I laughed so much that I had to hold on to the Land Rover to stop myself from sliding to the ground. Anyway, eventually I did help him out but he'd sunk in so much that his wellies didn't come out with him and he had to walk back across the field in his socks. He still can't see why I found it so amusing.

After the pace of summer, the bad weather of winter is a welcome relief. Some days I have the valley all to myself. A chance to do those jobs which have been waiting for a quiet spell. A chance to get soaking wet through too, day after day. A chance to get so cold you can't feel your fingers, and your face glows like a brazier when you finally get home and warm up. And when it snows, it SNOWS. Sometimes I can't get anywhere near my office, even in the Land Rover. More than once I have had to walk over a mile through deep drifts to get there.

Sometimes when the roads are icy I spend hours rescuing motorists who are stuck. Towing them up the hill to the gritted main road. I could make a fortune if I charged them. I could also be doing better things with my time. Why don't they stay at home when the roads are bad?

Uncontrolled moorland fires can be a nightmare. The last big fire burned on the moorland of Bleaklow for seven days. At one point there were four helicopters working, dropping water on to the burning heather and smouldering peat. We worked from early morning till evening, in the heat and smoke, pumping water, beating out flames and digging fire breaks, going home looking like coal miners. We were all completely tired out. The fire brigade's training and equipment wasn't appropriate for a moorland fire burning two miles from the nearest road but we stayed, working with the National Trust Wardens, the keepers and the North West Water people. How could we walk away? We do it for the sake of conservation to save the habitat of the ground nesting moorland birds and for the fact that if we did nothing we would lose all credibility.

We'll never know how that fire started, it could have been arson or a carelessly dropped cigarette, but for all our efforts trying to put it out, all we were ever able to do was stop it from spreading too widely. Even so it covered an area of about one square kilometre. That's like fifty football pitches. The fire would be burning still had the weather not changed to rain at the weekend. Wet weekends aren't all bad.

I drive the Argocart. Its main uses are transporting equipment and for fire fighting. It's a Canadian manufactured eight-wheeled, amphibious, go anywhere sort of vehicle. Forget your Land Rovers, this is eight-wheel all drive, which means each wheel has got its own source of power; as long as I've got one wheel on the ground, I can keep it going. I

think, considering the kind of places we take it to, that I'm the only one mad enough to drive it. I was once going down a hill so steep I had to stand on the dashboard just to stay in it.

I can put up to sixty gallons of water on the back and it's got a high pressure pump, so we can hose down the fires. I was once going to a fire in it with Geoff Howe, we were driving across the moor and there were flames shooting up into the sky and Geoff said to me, "I can't half smell petrol."

He felt that it was all wet underneath, so we lifted the floor and there was a big pool of liquid, six feet by four feet wide and about an inch deep. And we were charging towards a fire. A pipe had been broken and no one had told us, they had tried to fix it with an Elastoplast and five gallons of petrol leaked under the floor.

I was once working on a fire, it was up on Kinder and had been burning for several days. We were digging trenches around it to stop it spreading. This particular morning I was up on my own, a friend of mine was a JP and he was in court that morning but said he would join me up on Kinder at 2pm.

As I was up there I saw this sight coming towards me. It was an old gentleman on a bicycle. I would say he was at least seventy-five years old, he had on a navy blue pinstripe suit, a collar and tie and a flat cap. He looked like something straight out of a Lowry painting. He did three circuits around me and then vanished. I don't know where he came from or where he went, we were 2000ft up and at least three miles from the nearest road.

A couple of hours later my friend arrived and I asked him if he had seen anything strange.

"You mean that bloke on that bike."

I was relieved he had seen him, I thought I was going mad. We then checked for his tyre tracks, which we spotted, so it must have happened. Since then we have just referred to him as the 'Phantom Cyclist of Kinder.'

JUST PART OF THE JOB
Rangers to the Rescue

I am part of the Edale Mountain Rescue Team, it is the busiest team in the park. In 1997 we had eighty-six calls. We have a large group of volunteer rescuers who don't get paid a thing for doing a very difficult job, they even put their own petrol in their cars. The volunteers need to be in good physical shape and well trained. We train once a fortnight.

When my beeper goes I can guarantee that if I need them, I could have thirty rescuers gathered within twenty minutes. On some occasions I have had up to a hundred rescuers together within half an hour. The first job you have to do when a rescue call comes in, is to do your detective work. If it's a fixed incident, where somebody has fallen and has broken up on the floor, you know where they are so you can go and get them or I could call for an RAF Rescue Helicopter to the scene. If however it is someone missing, you have to work out a plan to find them.

The first thing you need to do is find a starting point. This can be a last sighting of the missing person or, if they came in a car, we find their car and start from there. When we have a starting point we try and work out the route they most probably took, we will call out the team and start searching. We have a highly trained pack of search and rescue dogs for such incidents. These dogs are trained differently to the police dogs. A police dog will follow a trail with its nose down. Our dogs walk with their nose in the air searching for a scent. They can pick up a scent from over a mile away, and once they get one, they will zoom in on it.

There is a variety of reasons why people get into difficulties. It's either stupidity, bad luck, bad weather, equipment failure and sometimes it can be pathetic leadership. Some youth club leaders and scout masters can be a danger to themselves and their group. It can be that a blizzard is about to swallow us up and we will advise them not to go above Kinder. But no, 'I have a mountain leadership certificate' they will say and they wear these things like a St Christopher. I have no choice but to offer stern words in some circumstances.

Easter is a bad time for it. Vicars and Youth Leaders will come up at the first sign of spring and off they go. I once had a whole youth club in trouble up there. Out of forty kids, thirty had hypothermia. We took them down to the centre at Edale and tried to bring them all round. The kids just don't have the metabolism of an adult. They are very good at absorbing food, which is great for a while, but they don't have a second wind. They don't have the mental attitude to pace themselves, they will be all running about then they will find themselves up on Kinder, knackered, with not enough energy to get back.

The Park can be a very serious place, I have had several people die on me. You have to put up with it. I once had a fourteen year old boy die in my arms, he was about the same age as my own lad at the time, so it makes you think a bit. My wife said I was very quiet that night.

Some people think mountain rescue is a macho job. You know the type of thing, flashing blue lights and high drama. They think there's some sort of glory in it. But it's not really like that at all. Many of the rescues are in remote places, in bad weather or at night when there's nobody about to see what's happening. Some incidents have a happy conclusion, like when you find missing walkers - safe and well. Others can be really distressing.

Every incident though has one essential element - that of surprise. It doesn't matter how often you've been involved in rescues or searches, they all start with surprise. This can be an annoying thing. It would be much easier if you knew when a rescue was likely to happen. You could make arrangements and postpone things so they didn't cause any problems. But of course, it doesn't work like that. Sure, sometimes you might guess that an incident was likely on a particularly bad-weather day, but you're nearly always wrong. Incidents usually happen when you least expect them - like on pleasant, sunny days.

I hate interruptions in the middle of a meal, especially when I'm enjoying something for the first time. I'd never eaten haggis before and was delighted when I found it to my liking. Then the telephone rang. Annoyed, I shouted to my teenage son to answer it,

seeing as it was nearly always for him. But this time it wasn't. The call was for assistance at an incident. My wife put my meal away in the warming oven ready for my return.

A young lad, out walking with his parents, had found a bike chained to a tree at a woodland fringe near a limestone crag. Nothing unusual in that of course, but like all young lads he began to explore and to his horror came across the body of a youth. It soon became obvious that the youth had been climbing solo on the crag, without ropes or protection and had fallen into the trees below. After the police made their observations and a doctor certified death, we carried his body in silence to an ambulance. It always seems worst when death happens to a young person.

When I eventually returned home, my son was on the telephone as usual. This time though I didn't complain, thinking how lucky I was to have him here unlike the poor parents of the dead youth. My wife brought the haggis out of the oven but I had lost my appetite by then.

From Edale we patrolled up on to the high, wild, plateau of Kinder Scout. It was a long patrol, bitterly cold, just before Christmas, a blanket of snow sapping the strength from tired legs. At times the weather on Kinder can be very cruel. At the end of this particularly unpleasant day we were called out to help recover a body. A woman had committed suicide.

She had simply stayed out on the top all night without adequate protection from the cold and had died of hypothermia.

So we put our wet boots back on and set off to face the winter again. It was pitch black when we finally struggled back up on to the plateau. Soon there was quite a crowd of rangers and policemen at the scene, standing around, waiting for the police doctor to come and confirm death, before anything could be done. It was a very surreal situation. The woman's body was covered in a fine layer of frost and stiff as a board. Almost as an antidote to the tragedy of the scene, people were nonchalant, even laughing and joking. Many of them had been to incidents like this before. Although the sadness of the circumstances was not lost to them, it was important to stay detached. It was just part of the job. The carry-off was very difficult, but at least we could go home and forget about it. Easier said than done.

It was the end of May and the day of the Castleton Garland. Despite the heavy traffic, there was sunshine and a carnival atmosphere amongst the crowds that thronged through the village. Excited families queued for admittance to the renowned show-caves that are peppered around Castleton. Some of the more energetic visitors trudged up the steep path leading to the ruins of Peveril Castle where there is a glorious view of the valley below.

Below the castle, four young men climbed over a fence and began playing about on the grassy slopes leading to the towering cliffs above Peak Cavern. The youths had been drinking so perhaps caution was blunted by carefree minds. Two of them ran down the slope to recover a football.

Peak Cavern has the largest cave entrance in Britain and the cliffs above rise to about two hundred feet. Crowds queuing for admittance to the cave watched in horror as the two youths plunged from above, falling into a rocky ravine below.

Probably wondering why their friends hadn't returned, the other two youths went to investigate. The slope leading down to the cliffs is convex. There is no defined edge. No real stopping point. To picture this, imagine trying to run down the side of a huge whale. As the youths progressed, they reached a decisive point where their balance could no longer be maintained. Unable to retreat and unable to stand upright they tumbled and also plunged into the dreadful chasm.

The police requested ranger assistance with extricating the bodies and five rangers using mountain rescue techniques recovered them. It was a profoundly sad and difficult job - even worse for the full-time ranger when he later attended the inquest and met the distraught families of the dead men. He said at the inquest that he had tested the hillside by abseiling down part of it. Even with the security of a rope, he found himself suddenly

unable to stand upright at what first appeared to be a harmless position on the shoulder of the slope.

There was no counselling in those days; we each dealt with the tragedy in our own way.

My friends sometimes say why do you do it? I must admit there are times when I wonder why. I mean, not everyone would be willing to give up a free Sunday every fortnight to be a part-time ranger would they? It's certainly not for the money; I could be earning more assembling counterfeit Teletubbies in some Third World sweatshop. But I'm office-bound throughout the week so I really look forward to my weekend as a ranger - working outdoors and meeting people.

The best thing about the job is not knowing what might happen when you're on duty. There might be poachers to deal with or some incident that really gets the adrenaline moving like a rescue or a fire. Sometimes the job is an absolute joy. When the sun is shining and you're meeting lots of agreeable people. Times like when I've just helped somebody find the best way across the moor or explained some local feature that they weren't aware of. Kids are the best. They have such natural wonder about the countryside. The look on their faces if you can show them something out of the ordinary is worth all the effort.

Of course, there are times when I wonder what the hell am I doing. Like when I'm struggling against a gale force wind, bent double across some fearful moor, lashed by torrential rain, underclothes so wet I feel as if I'm wrapped in cling-film. My legs ache. My feet ache. Even my head aches from the unrelenting, biting wind. I squelch through peat bog. Feet, already wet, become stuck in the stagnating mire. I struggle to escape. It sucks me down. I struggle again. Eventually my feet come out with the sound of a slurp and a plop. The stink of the rotten bog clogs the air as the ooze settles once more to await its next victim. My legs are now coated in a mess resembling black porridge.

When shelter is eventually found for a lunch break, I discover that my coffee is cold. My sandwiches, so lovingly prepared by my wife, are now a grey, sodden mess. Eating them is like chewing wet papier-mâché. Then I think, " Why aren't I at home sat in front of the bloody fire like normal people?"

Sean Prendergast

John Howson

David Gwynn-Jones

Di Reynolds

John Anfield

John Polter

Karen Harrison

Neville Care

P Sutcliffe

Matthew Capper

Mrs Irene Wright

M J Dannatt

Mrs S Ashton

S Helliwell

A M Farmer

Haydn Tanner

I W Taylor

Jo Barber

Ann Robinson

John Youatt

Neil Broadbent

Ian Hurst

T D Hanley

Mrs S M Cook

D W & G C Jenkins

Philip Shaw

R Slack

Roy Stringer

Lynn Burrow

John Fielding

Neil Hanshaw

D M Coulson

Andy McGraw

Sara Harrop

Margaret Haddon

Kenneth Robinson

G McDonald

R J Tuccillo

D Dalrymple-Smith

Miss G Heathcote

Chris Webb

Paul Herschell

A Gerrard

C P Hewson

Mrs J M Alderson

Graham Hahn

Elaine Quinn

G A Plant

Nicky Crewe

Kate Holden

E Wood

D Roebuck

Richard Church

John Thompson

Tanya Clark-Bennett

Robert Davey

I R Thistlewaite

Andy Valentine

Paul Flannigan

A W Smith

Margaret Black

D Kirwen

G R Mottram

Dave Murphy

Geoff Frost

Nadine Ajiba

Ron McLaughlin

J Wheeler

Harry Ball

A D Leadbeater

Jeffery Cheetham

P A McMahon

T J Ward

Carol Renshaw

K Eastwood

Gordon Miller

Caroline Donovan

L Ash